T0064314

THE
POWER
TO BE HOLY

DEACON BERNARD R. SWIFT D. MIN

Order this book online at www.trafford.com
or email orders@trafford.com

Most Trafford titles are also available at major online book retailers.

Print information available on the last page.

ISBN: 978-1-4907-6432-0 (sc)
ISBN: 978-1-4907-6433-7 (hc)
ISBN: 978-1-4907-6434-4 (e)

Library of Congress Control Number: 2015913252

Scripture quotations marked NASB are taken from the *New American Standard Bible®*,
Copyright © 1960, 1962, 1963, 1968, 1971, 1972, 1973, 1975, 1977, 1995 by The
Lockman Foundation. Used by permission.

Trafford rev. 08/14/2015

 www.trafford.com

North America & international
toll-free: 1 888 232 4444 (USA & Canada)
fax: 812 355 4082

ROMAN CATHOLIC
DIOCESE *of* **ORANGE**
OFFICE OF THE BISHOP
13280 CHAPMAN AVENUE, GARDEN GROVE, CA 92840

May 5, 2015

Deacon Bernie Swift
151 W. Hillside St.
La Habra, CA 90631

Dear Bernie,

Thank you for the opportunity to review your manuscript "Be Holy". Enclosed is the manuscript with some grammatical corrections/suggestions. I would like to provide you with the following review for the manuscript:

Deacon Bernie Swift has provided us with a retreat in print. In this short booklet, he reminds us of the familiar words in which Jesus invites us to 'be perfect as our Father in heaven is perfect.' Deacon Swift utilizes Sacred Scripture and the Catechism of the Catholic Church to enlighten his work. Based on these strong foundations, he proceeds, in simple and practical terms, to outline for us the path to spiritual perfection.

I am grateful to him for the insights he has gained from his own ministry as a Deacon and spiritual reading. I pray that his readers will be inspired in their own journey toward perfection and moved to greater spiritual depths through the wisdom that he has shared with us.

Thank you again for your ministry and dedication to study and prayer and please know of my prayer for a blessed Paschal season for you and your family.

Sincerely in Christ,

+Kevin W. Vann

Most Reverend Kevin W. Vann, J.C.D., D.D.
Bishop of Orange

KWV:mb

ACKNOWLEGEMENT

Deacon Bernie Swift,

Thank you for the opportunity to let me read your latest book, The Power to be Holy, prior to release. I believe this book is a gifted road map of spirituality and guidance that one can choose to use in bettering one's Christian life toward the goal of true salvation with our creator. I pray that I can apply the steps laid out so wonderfully in each of your chapters in my quest for achieving holiness. Thank you and may God through the gift of his son Jesus and the Holy Spirit continue to allow your writings to touch all those who are blessed in His name.

Sincerely,

Your friend in Christ,
Tom Keysor

CONTENTS

CONTENTS

CHAPTER 1

INTRODUCTION TO BE HOLY

Did you know of God's great love for us, He wants us to become "holy" as His beloved Son is holy? In essence, "perfect?" Therefore, anyone who follows Jesus in His footsteps can and should become holy as Jesus!

The Catechism of the Catholic Church ("C.C.C.") 2013 confirms this theological find, "All Christians in any state of walk of life are called to the fullness of Christian life and to the perfection of Christ." All are called to holiness; perfect as your Heavenly Father is perfect. Matthew 5:48, "So be perfect, just as your Heavenly Father is perfect." This is only in the Gospel of Matthew. However, Luke comes closest in 6:36, "Be merciful as your Father is merciful." Merciful is a feeling that comes from the heart to forgive someone. It ties in with holiness which requires forgiveness from the heart.

Don't let this scare you to say, "I am not Jesus. I can't be perfect." If we are followers of Jesus, we definitely can progress in becoming better persons and reach this fullness of life. We start with following in the steps of our good Lord Jesus.

As we delve through scripture, we find parts of Jesus' life that we can immitate. He wants us to love Him, his Father or neighbor or we can help our neighbor as Christ loved them and help them with shelter, food or clothing or visit people in hospitals and pray for them. Also, one can visit and pray for the prisoners and help them in any way you can. Then, by continual progress, we can pray for the poor souls in purgatory and all other people who are suffering and carrying heavy burdens and need a variety of helps.

As for suggestion at this time in asking God our Father for His help to do His will and ask for blessings for every action you do for every moment in your life. Also, ask Him to even sanctify you and bless you to lead a better life and to become someday holy as Jesus is holy. How we need the theological virtues to support us in holiness.

CHAPTER 2

FAITH

God as an infinite being who was never created, created male and female to His own image and likeness. He created people for Himself to be able to love them and then call them to live with Him for all eternity.

Who is this being who created man with all the faculties of a living God and placed them on earth to be for Himself? This God was a superior infinite being that created the entire universe with billions of stars, a sun and moon; galaxies that are interspersed so precisely that they function as clockwork, not running into each other or the earth to destroy it.

God is not only an infinite being, but He is also divine, holy and a perfect being. And he wants all of us to become perfect as the Heavenly Father. God knows man and He knows how much each person needed help in his living a good and happy life. So, he gave Moses the Ten Commandments and instituted baptism, a sacrament that would provide each person with the Holy Spirit.

This spirit provides each person with seven gifts of wisdom, understanding, counsel, fortitude, knowledge, piety, and the fear of the Lord our God. These are perfections formed within us to assist

us to love and worship God and love our neighbor and to enter into
eternal love and peace in Heaven. We can use these God-given gifts
in our daily life to help us make good decisions when it comes to
how to best live our lives in our faith to be happy and earn our way
into paradise.

There are many other gifts available from the Holy Spirit, but
some of us may decide not to desire these gifts. They take upon
themselves to decide what is good or bad and live a life according
to their own whims of desires to only give themselves a temporary
feeling of peace and happiness.

Many don't feel there is a purpose of life. They say that they will
lead a good life and be able to enter Heaven or a good place where
they will be happy. How wrong they could be! How can you not
believe in God?

1. Common sense dictates that there is some higher power. It
   could be something in your mind that you cannot express.
2. The creation of the earth and all the heavenly bodies that are
   still out in space that our telescopes cannot see.
3. Historically, the life of Christ that has been recorded by
   pagan historians to their kings.
4. Over one billion Catholics believe it could be about the same
   for other Christian faiths. Also, Muslims believe in God.

CHAPTER 3

HOPE

God places hope in his people through Abraham and Moses by increasing the race as sands of the sea. He also made a new covenant that cannot be broken as it was written in the hearts of people in Jeremiah. "But, this is the covenant which I will make with the house of Israel after those days," says the Lord. "I will place my law within them and write it upon their hearts; I will be their God and they shall be my people. No longer will they need to teach their friends and kinsmen how to know the Lord, for I will forgive their evildoings and remember their sin no more." This prophesy was fulfilled through Jesus Christ who established a new covenant of himself.

God himself came down from heaven as Jesus to suffer and die for our sins to remove them forever so we can enter paradise with God. In Peter 5:10, God promised, "The God of all grace who called you to this eternal glory though Christ will himself restore, confirm, strengthen and establish you after you have suffered a little. Naturally, all serious sins must be forgiven by God or through confession through a priest with absolution.

In Catechism of the Catholic Church 1818, "The virtue of hope . . . takes up the hopes that inspire men's activities and sustains him during times of abandonment. It opens up his heart in expectation of external beatitude. Buoyed up by hope, he is preserved from selfishness and led to the happiness that flows from charity."

Hope is the essence of God's love. Because God loves us so much, we know and feel that God will take care of us. He will never abandon us. We should never despair and feel that God will disappoint us if we are not worthy to be saved. No matter how sinful we may become, we know that God will always forgive us as he "thirsts" for our souls. One of the greatest sins is the sin of presumption whereby we believe we have already been forgiven with no further need of conversion. This can destroy hope.

We must thank God frequently for giving us life and time to repent our transgressions. Pray and thank God for everything we have received from him and live a good and hopeful, holy life.

CHAPTER 4

BEATITUDES

In a book, "A Do It At Home Retreat" written by Andre Ravier using the spiritual exercises by Saint Ignatius of Loyola p.p. 143-146, meditation on the Sermon on the Mount. Jesus asked the crowd to assemble near the shoreline. In His talk, Jesus will ask for the grace of understanding of the true life and the grace to follow him more closely.

Jesus will open this scripture of the beatitudes and begins with the Kingdom of God is theirs, the poor homeless, those who need help, those who are sick and those in prison will received help and blessings from Jesus as they are the nearest to the kingdom. All the beatitudes have the same trust. They all lead to the same group of people; the poor.

In essence, Jesus rewards those who are the poor and those who pray for them with joy and happiness. It is good and holy of those who can dwell in the beatitudes and receive the pleasure of joy and happiness for our meditation on them.

All his life, Jesus practices the beatitudes for the poor in spirit. Jesus refers to those who live humbly. They are the people who will follow humbly in the footsteps of Jesus Christ and the kingdom of Heaven is theirs.

In Matthew 25:40, Jesus explains the result of those who refuse to take care of the poor. "Amen, I say to you, whatever you did for the least brothers of mine, you did for me" and failure to provide for the hungry, thirsty, naked, ill, prisoner will result in eternal punishment. Our responsibility is serious. Failure to provide for the hungry will result in eternal punishment.

Jesus can only help the poor only through us. We become the hands and feet of our good Lord.

God does not condemn the materiality the rich. But, as God gives these gifts to us, we are responsible to share them with the less fortunate.

In Matthew 19:16-20, when a rich young man asked what he must do to gain eternal life? Jesus told him to, "Go sell what you have and give it to the poor." The young man could not do it. So, Jesus told his disciples in Matthew 19:23-24, "Amen, I say to you it will be hard for one who is rich to enter the kingdom of God. Again I say to you, it would be easier for a camel to pass through an eye of a needle that for one who is rich to enter the kingdom of heaven."

The soul that can accept Jesus must be empty and prove free of clutter or concerns and totally open to accommodate the King of Kings.

We can now approach God with empty hands, open soul and great desire to love him as he want to be loved. Now God can find a place to live. Jesus enters and changes our loves. We become one with God. And, with God, we can go forward with confidence. We become a burning flame that can change the world.

CHAPTER 5

HUMILITY

In the book of Revelation, St. Ignatius Loyola takes being humble and modifies it in three degrees or three levels.

The first degree is that the individual would observe the laws of God in all things. He would not consider breaking any of the commandments of God or the church that binds under mortal sin even if it would be to gain the whole world or even if his life depended on it.

The second degree is that the person would have attained a status of soul wherein he does not seek riches, honor, long life, etc. He would not consider committing one venial sin; not even for the entire creation, not even at the risk of saving his life. He loves God with a very high degree of love.

The third degree of humility is that the person would choose poverty rather than riches; humiliation like Christ rather than honors, be a man of no account, a fool for Christ also willing to accept hardship and pain and rejoice in them for the love of God and then praise be given to his Divine Majesty.

The first degree of humility stems around the person who is considered a very good Catholic. He lives a good life and he abides by all the laws and sacraments of the church

The second degree Catholic, as far as humility is concerned, has attained a high state of living God's word and does commune with God frequently during the day. He is living in God's word in order to be one with God and one with His people. His neighbor comes before he does and makes sure they are well taken care of. Any free time he has is devoted to others who need his help and guidance in leading a good and happy life.

The third degree includes the first and second degrees, but adds that he would have poverty rather than riches, humiliation with Christ rather than honors or glory and choose to be a man of no account and a fool for Christ.

The paragraphs below will give you a good indication how the apostles lived in bringing the message of Christ to the people. St. Paul expresses it clearly of the degree of humility required in this category in 1st Corinthians 4:10-14. "We are fools on Christ's account, but you are wise wise in Christ! We are weak, but you are strong! You are held in honor, but we in disrespect." To this very hour, we go hungry and thirsty. We are poorly clad and roughly treated. We wander about homeless and we toil, working with our own hands. When we are reviled, we bless; when persecuted, we endure; when slandered, we respond gently. We have become like the world's rubbish, the scum of all, to this very moment.

CHAPTER 6

SUPERNATURAL LOVE

Spiritual love will take on a different characteristic then ordinary or natural love. Natural love is a feeling between two persons that says, "I like living in your company and being able to accept all of their idiosyncrasies, good and bad habits, their beliefs in something or in God, also his likes and dislikes. Spiritual love goes much beyond this. It is love generated by the Holy Spirit. This love comes directly from the heart and it embodies everything that is pleasing and loving to God our savior. It takes on the characteristics of "agape" love. This love is true love, holy love, love unconditional, and has no bounds.

Supernatural love accepts all hurts, shame, suffering, discord and humiliation. It can live joyfully with any handicap or burden. The reason is the Lord supplies the endurance, the strength, the wisdom to understand and accept the conflicts and problems committed by the natural man.

A case in point of the power and strength of spiritual love is: A husband was an alcoholic, abusive and unfaithful. What can a wife do? There is Alcoholics Anonymous that can help. But the husband goes, then returns and then reverts to being alcoholic and continues his bad habits. The wife considered to be a gift of God. The woman only with natural love might seek a divorce. However, as the marriage took place in church and both husband and wife made a pledge to God for a permanent bond. What happens is God can pour into the woman through Jesus and the Holy Spirit with love. This could definitely hold the marriage together through supernatural love that can help the woman to carry the burden just like Jesus who had to carry His cross. This gives the woman strength and wisdom from God to be patient and to continue to carry her cross as a test for her love of God. In Romans 5:3-5, we are confident even over our afflictions, even knowing well that afflictions rise to endurance and endurance gives proof of our faith and a proved faith gives grounds for hope. Nor this hope deludes us; the love of God has been poured over in our hearts by the Holy Spirit, whom we have received.

The husband never changed as the habit was so deeply ingrained. The wife continues praying for his conversion. However, the wife can separate and by the grace of God the husband may become converted. The wife then could join her husband and live together.

In the Catholic faith, divorce is not recommended. However, a separation may resolve the problem.

CHAPTER 7

SUPERNATURAL LOVE II

Our family depends highly on supernatural love. Many incidents were prayed for and recovered. Some of the following:

1. My wife had a beautiful golden necklace and put it in a dresser drawer that had a trash can directly under the drawer. She thought it slipped off the top of the drawer and fell into the trash can. She searched the whole can and then she got the trash bag that was before in the can. She looked through the whole bag and could not find it. Then, I asked my son to look through several other drawers. In the meantime, I called upon the Holy Spirit. In two minutes, we found the necklace in the second drawer. My wife was greatly pleased.

2. Anytime I misplaced something of value, I call on the Holy Spirit and I find it in only a couple of minutes.

3. When I began to worry about someone or something, I call upon the Spirit of God and I place the problem in God's hands and the worry stops.

Actually, we receive the power directly from God who transmits the power through Jesus to the Holy Spirit. Living in the Spirit makes life a lot easier and more joyful. This is all God given. We can only do what God has permitted us to do.

In our earthly living, we have many faults and wrong desires. We have to pray to eliminate them, as many as we can, of our bad habits and spend more time in prayer to be able to grasp as many of the gifts of God as we possibly can.

God tells us that we must love Him with our whole heart, soul, all our mind and strength to love our neighbors as ourselves. You can gather from this that God wants all of us at all times and He wants all our love; not only for Him, but our enemies as well. This takes a lot of time to share our love with not only God, but all the people we come in contact with.

When Jesus was about to leave his apostles to go to His Father in heaven, he told them in John 14:16, "And I will ask the Father, and he will give you another advocate to help you and be with you always ~ the Spirit of truth which the world cannot accept because it is neither sees or knows it. But, you know it." Then, in 14:18, "Because I will come to you." Then, in 14:19, "You will see Me because I live and you will live." Then, 20-21, "On that day, you will realize that I am in my Father and you are in Me and I in you. Whosoever has My commandments observes them and is the one who loves Me. And, whoever loves Me will be loved by My Father and I will love him and reveal myself to him. Then in John 14:23, "Whoever loves Me will keep My word and My Father will love him and he will come to him and make Our dwelling with him."

The love of God the Father is amazing that the trinity (Father, Son, and Holy Spirit) will live within all of us (and we must be baptized) and testify of God's great love for us.

After being sinners or indifferent to God's great love for us, God comes to us, and God promised us He would never leave us. We could leave Him or deny Him and God will stay with such persons until death. God said He would never abandon us. God may lay dormant or just let the Holy Spirit be His advocate until the denier comes to his senses and asks God for forgiveness.

CHAPTER 8

BE HOLY

Continuing the exhortation of C.C.C. 2013, we see "In order to reach this perfection, the faithful to use the strength dealt out to them for Christ's gift so that doing the will of the Father in everything, they may whole-heartedly devote their selves to the glory of God and to the service of their neighbor." Thus, the holiness of the people of God will grow in fruitful abundance as is clearly shown in the history of the Church through the lives of so many Saints.

We can see that this gift is given to many of the Saints, but this gift is also made available to all who would want it. Even if this intimate union be given to some special person, it does not mean that all of us can get this gift from God as he will make it available to all who desire this beautiful gift.

In C.C.C. 2015, "Perfection calls for the way of the cross. There is no holiness without renunciation or spiritual battle. Spiritual progress entails the ascesis, self disapline and mortification that gradually lead to living in the peace and joy of the Beatitudes." In other words, we must conquer our will to the will of God and deny ourselves of all worldly facets of living to live Christ like. We then begin to live the Beatitudes as expressed by Jesus. This is where the battle lies in our desires of the world and to cater to them instead of the will of God.

Actually, we have battles fairly frequently on worldly matters. We can have conflicts, disbeliefs, or say it is impossible. We know that there is nothing impossible with God. We can call upon Him for strength. He will give it to us. We have to do the rest ~ like prayer, denial of worldly possessions, and petitions to God to help you to be holy or at least to become a better person.

CHAPTER 9

WORK OF THE HOLY
SPIRIT – DIVINITY

Let us begin with the sanctifier who is the Holy Spirit, the third person of the Blessed Trinity. He is the power to justify us, to cleanse us from our sins, to open our hearts to God through His son Jesus Christ, through Baptism.

We know in baptism, "we die with Christ and die to sin and alive to God in Christ." In C.C.C. 1988, "God gave himself to us through the Spirit. By the participation of the Spirit, we become one in the divine nature and are divinized." As we call out during the Eucharistic celebration during the Mass, "By the mystery of the "water and wine, may we come to share in the divinity of Christ who humbled Himself to share in our humanity."

As baptized Christians, we live in a holy and divinized state. We have the Holy Spirit at our finger tips to talk to and ask for anything we need and the good Lord promised He will do it.

In accordance of C.C.C. 1989, the first work of the grace of the Holy Spirit is conversion, effecting justification as per Jesus Christ. Man turns toward God and away from sin. Justification not only removes sin, but also the sanctification and renewal of the man.

Also, with justification, faith, hope and charity are poured into our hearts and obedience to the divine will.

God has allowed us the freedom to accept or reject God's will and plan for us. If we do not plan to accept all facets of justification of the Lord by self denial of all worldly tasks and pleasures and turn away from sin, we will live a life of mediocrity, resulting in the loss of eternal life in heaven.

The greatest work of the Holy Spirit comes from the graces of justification given by God to His son Jesus who then permits the Holy Spirit to grant us the graces of sanctification to further our blessings to become one with our beloved Lord our God. We could then enjoy a significant change in our lifestyle and experience a joy inexpressible to be in paradise with his beloved.

Living a separate life with a family would be difficult as much of the small talk would be eliminated. My joy would be my Lord and my God with loving embrace and enjoying the essence of sanctification.

In C.C.C. 1996, "Our justification comes from the grace of God. Grace is *favor*, the free and undeserved help that God gives us to respond to his call to become children (heirs)of God, adoptive sons and daughters, partakers of the divine nature and of eternal life." It is a participation in the life of God.

This vocation "of the life of God" is freely awarded to people selected by God.

In. C.C.C. 2000, "Sanctifying grace is a habitual gift, a supernatural disposition that perfects the soul itself to enable it to live with God, to act by his love."

There are also actual graces which are God's actual interventions. But, as we know, God is always present and available to help us. Without Him, we could not be able to do anything.

There are special favors called "charismas" or "favors." C.C.C. 2782 shows "God, indeed, who has predestined us to adoption as his sons, has conformed us to the glorious Body of Christ. So then you who have become sharers in Christ are appropriately called "Christs."

No one knows what pertains to God except the Spirit of God. We have not received the spirit of the world, but the Spirit that is from God so that we may understand that things freely given us by God. And, we may speak about them not with the words taught by human wisdom, but with words taught by the Spirit describing spiritual realities in spiritual terms.

Now, the natural person does not accept what pertains to the Spirit of God, for to him it is foolishness and he cannot understand it, because it is judged spiritually. The spiritual person, however, can judge everything but is not subject to judgment by anyone. As we have been accepted by God, we dwell in His spiritual life and we can understand and judge others who are in the natural world and cannot understand us as we are in the realm of God's judgment. This exempts us and gives us the privilege of knowing what God is trying to tell us in scripture.

Natural persons cannot see or understand us at times as we try to explain scripture. They think it is foolish and stop listening to us as we begin to enter into God's world. This world goes beyond comprehension for the natural man.

If we are evangelizing, we need to be careful with the Neophytes who are just starting to learn and understand scripture. If he wants to understand how we can commune with God and His Holy Spirit, we can tell him what steps and time to be able to move in to the supernatural spiritual world.

The natural man would have to begin with trying to follow in the footsteps of Jesus. Go through his life living with the same humiliations and suffering that Jesus went through. Acts 1:8, "But you will receive power when the Holy Spirit has come upon you." This was the day the Holy Spirit came as tongues of fire upon the apostles of Jesus that gave them the power to go throughout the world (at that time about 2000 years ago) to evangelize the world. However, the Holy Spirit is available now. As we live in Jesus and Jesus lives in us, we can call upon Jesus to give us the power now to evangelize the part of the world that we live in. We can ask Jesus to give us the knowledge, wisdom and strength to talk to our family and friends, including our neighbors and anyone we come in contact.

The indwelling of the abundance and power of the Holy Spirit, all problems and tests are solvable. With God's help, nothing is impossible. We only need to ask our Lord to help us. The problem could be solved before it is asked.

The Holy Spirit also blesses and sanctifies us, (2 Thes. 2:15b) because God chose you as firstfruits for salvation through sanctification by the Holy Spirit and through belief in truth."

We have received this great blessing through Jesus from God not only for us to understand, but also for others to whom we are trying to explain the Gospel so they understand,

In John 16:13-14, "But when He, the Spirit of truth, comes, he will guide you to all truth. He will not speak on his own; he will speak what he hears and will declare to you the things that are coming. He will glorify me because he will take what is mine and declare it to you."

In 1st Corinthians, St. Paul is telling us that with the assistance of the Paraclete that who will guide us to all truth and he will glorify him when the Paraclete repeats what Paul said.

Needs strong desire and deep prayer to progress.

CHAPTER 10

PRAYER

Prayer is essentially communion with God. One should in our deepest devotion should want to lift himself up to convene with God, our lovely Father. Being children of God, he expects prayer primarily for petitions and appreciation or everything He has given us.

We, as sinners, must shed all our sins of clandestine affairs and controlled anger and lust. Prayer is a gift from God. We know how the apostles asked Jesus to teach them how to pray. And, Jesus answered to each of them, the "Our Father," which contains important parts of how to live our lives with our neighbors and friends.

Prayer is the most powerful way we can approach our Father who dwells within us and awaiting our call to him at any time during the day or night. We baptized believers have this great opportunity lying at our fingertips who loves us so much and is thirsting for our souls to spend eternity with Him.

Jesus said repeatedly and with loving desire to ask Him whatever you need and He will grant it for you.

We need to talk to Jesus and our Father and tell them of our problems and needs by praying from the depths of our heart and explain (even though they already know our needs before we tell them) what we really need to move us in our spiritual life. Tell Jesus how much you love Him, appreciate what He has given us (everything we have), and now you want to change your life so you could love and appreciate and thank Him more deeply then before. You want to grow in holiness.

Your growth in holiness will have to take on a new life, a conversion from simply daily tasks to greater efforts in conveying God's message to His children and to help them to act upon their messages; that is, to live them as Jesus did.

CHAPTER 11

PRAYER II

As the Holy Spirit is the giver of gifts and can help you to apply them to you, one needs to pray to Him. He will help you to supernatural or spiritual living. As we are all children (heirs) of God, we have available all of God's possessions. We have a much greater power that is realized within us for victorious living and fruitful witnessing for our Lord Jesus Christ. We will be able to experience joy and happiness beyond our comprehension as we begin to live our spiritual life. We may lose some desire for sinful pleasures. We will have better control of our feelings or anger, slander, lust and envy. We will experience more happiness, Love and joy in our lives. We will enjoy being more positive instead of being critical and a complainer. We won't be losing anything.

In 1st Corinthians 3:16-18, "Do you not know you are the temple of God and *that* the Spirit of God dwells in you? [17] If anyone destroys God's temple, God will destroy that person. For the temple of God, which you are, is holy." Our temple which is inside of us is holy, yet are we living a holy life?

How can we live a real holy life?

1. We must have a strong desire to live it.
2. We must repent all our faults and sins and confess them and have them absolved.
3. We need to receive the Eucharist more frequently than once a week.
4. As we live in the world, we must work to earn a living, lean our home and garden, and possibly take care of our family.
5. We need to help others; homeless, feed the hungry, needy, clothing, visit those in prison and those who are sick.
6. Take time to pray as written in prior chapters.
7. We need to begin living our spiritual life.
8. As witnesses, we need to evangelize the scripture and be able to explain it to others and to have them able to live it.

Ephesians 6:18-20, ". . . with all prayer and supplications, pray at every opportunity in the Spirit. To that end, be watchful with all perseverance and supplication for all of the holy ones and also for Me, that speech may be given me to open my mouth, to make known with boldness and mystery of the Gospel for which I am an ambassador in chains to that I may have the courage to speak as I must."

Paul, in this last discourse, is speaking of battle with the evil one where he might have to speak his last words from chains. He's talking about the struggle not with flesh and blood, but with principalities, with the powers, world rulers and the present darkness and the evil spirit that roams the world.

CHAPTER 12

GOD'S WILL AND PLAN

We know that God is perfect. His plan for each person is different. The road or plan for us is not impossible. The plan probably can be difficult in parts of His plan for us, but it is not impossible. Besides, God would help us carry it out.

God loves us. This would be beyond description. We know that God would follow us and stay with us until the last minute of our lives. He would try to help us over our bumps and gives us graces to reduce any punishment that any of our sins would require.

We must search out God's will by asking Him if we are going in the right direction or we may be slipping and going off course. We may have certain problems that we need to overcome. God will provide our answers. He will steer us in the right direction with the Holy Spirit and counselors.

God will provide us with ideas, visions, wisdom, power, personnel, even way to finance a project as needed. We also need to communicate with Jesus obeying His commandments and beatitudes and to help us in receiving the will of God. Tell Jesus that you will give your deepest love and sacrifice your life for His cause.

Our problem may lie with the considerable din of noise that disturbs our listening for God's response to our requests. However, we need some quiet place to confer with our loving savoir. In John 2:17b, "but whoever does the will of God remains forever."

May God fill us with His love for Him and for others. Ephesians 4:17-19, "Instructions for Christian Living ~ that Christ may dwell in your hearts through faithfulness. And I pray that you, being rooted and grounded in love, may have the strength to comprehend with all the holy ones what is the breadth and length, the height and the depth, and to know the love of Christ that surpasses knowledge so that you may be filled with all the fullness of God."

St. Paul is asking the Father to strengthen his belief in Christ; that the love of God may permeate through Christ the love of God and Christ will expand throughout all the people in His churches.

Talk to God on all matters, particularly what His will is for you. He will provide an answer ~ though it may be indirect, though it may be from some other source or some other person ~ you will get an answer.

In John 14: 20-23, Jesus is telling his apostles that he will soon be leaving. "On that day you will realize that I am in my Father, and you are in me and I in you. Whoever has my commandments and observes them is the one loves me. And he who loves me will be loved by my Father, and I will love him and reveal myself to him(23b)and, we will come to him and make our dwelling with him."

Jesus is telling us that he and the Father will dwell within us and He will give us the power over our weakness and remove our sins. They will give us the fullness of holiness. We now have the holy disposition to move forward in the people we meet. We have new spirit that we can bear witness to the events in scripture to them and explain to them and conceive them into the fold of Christianity, plus pray for them. Ephesians 1:5, God chose us in Him.

Before the foundations of the world to be holy and without blemish before Him, God "thirsts" for our souls from the beginning of time. Let's not disappoint Him.

CHAPTER 13

SUPERNATURAL LIVING

In Philippians 4:11, 13, "Not that I say this because of need, for I have learned in whatever situation, to be self sufficient. I have the strength for everything though Him who powers me." St. Paul seems to be satisfied in everything that he did in his evangelical work of the new world. This is supported by the strength provided by the Holy Spirit.

Satisfaction is a physical characteristic that is absolutely amenable for all of us who are living in Christ. Jesus will supply us everything we need to continue our work for the Holy Spirit. God has given us everything we have and everything we need to continue out work primarily in evangelizing. We don't need fame and fortune or titles to impress anyone. We only need to impress God for all He has given us. God already knows all He had given us; we don't need fanfare or important names or titles. God loves us and encourages us to continue our work.

1 Peter 2:9-10, "But you are a chosen race, a royal priesthood, a holy nation, a people of His own, so that you may announce the praises of Him who called you out of darkness into his wonderful light. Once you were not a people, but now you are God's people;

you had not received mercy, but now you have received mercy." This applies to God's people now.

We are the chosen people who were baptized into the death and resurrection of Christ and we will proceed through the life of Christ. We will move from darkness into the light. We were once not a people, but now we are the chosen people of God through His divine mercy we have become one with Christ our Lord.

This is living as God wants us to live. In John 4:24, Jesus told the woman at the well that "God is a Spirit and those who worship Him must worship in spirit and truth." We know that we have the Holy Spirit of the Lord dwelling inside us. We can worship Him and ask Him whatever we need. He will give it to us. Also, whatever problem we have or any decision we have to make, just call the Holy Spirit and He will help you.

An interesting situation happened today. My daughter who had multiple sclerosis in phase III was calling for "someone" to help her relieve some of the great pain she suffers every night in her feet. She made calls for someone to help her in the nursing home. There was no response. Finally, she called the Holy Spirit to help her get help. In a few minutes, someone appeared to help her.

Let us ask in the Holy Spirit in most of our work or home or at a business for help in whatever we need. Start living and worshipping in the spirit.

Are we the children of God?

In Romans 8:14, "For those who are led by the Spirit of God are the children of God." For you did not receive the spirit of slavery to fall back into fear, but you received the spirit of adoption through which to cry "Abba, Father."

The Spirit itself bears witness with our spirit that we are children of God. And, children, their heirs, heirs of God and joint heirs with Christ, if only we suffer with Him, may be glorified with Him. We not only have a newer and closer relationship with God being His direct children, but also a new relationship with Jesus to suffer with Him and be glorified with Jesus.

Now we can work with Jesus and His Father in a closer relationship and get things done better, quicker, and more enjoyable, plus the added graces we receive if we offer up everything we do to be blessed and sanctified. Always remember to ask the good Lord to sanctify us at the same time.

CHAPTER 14

WE CAN DO GREATER WORKS

Jesus tells in John 14:13-14; "Amen, amen. I say to you, whoever believes in me will do the works that I do, and do greater one than these, because I am going to the Father. And, whatever you ask in my name, I will do, so that the Father may be glorified in the Son. If you ask anything of me in my name, I will do it."

This is a hard saying as only some of the Saints have been able to do these things. However, this saying is offered to all baptized Christians who follow Jesus. To accomplish such a feat would require a lay person to have a great faith and depth and love of God burning in his heart beyond measure and a deep desire to help others as God would condescend to permit this to happen. But, we lay people can do numerous things to help the poor and needy by evangelizing them, provide food, clothing, and shelter and visit the sick and those in prison.

This report is a separate charism just to show the power of the Holy Spirit. It has been gained by considerable reading and good books, Christian literature and watching T.V. Further research revealed that the practices of healing were being accomplished by the Christian lay persons and evangelists and preachers.

Repeatedly, Jesus tells us and shows us how to manifest healing by deep prayer, exhortation to remove pain and suffering and touch to the afflicted spot then to thank the Lord for the healing of some of the sick persons.

Normally when a large group of people approach the altar only some of them are cured as God is the sovereign authority of hope to heal. Some must suffer longer and only God would know the reason for that.

All lives of healing take place from simple headaches to torn muscles and torn bodies.

Authority to heal comes strictly from God through Jesus Christ by the Holy Spirit. Jesus tells us in Jn. 14:13-14, "Amen, Amen I say to you, whoever believes in me will do the works I do, and do greater works than that."

The material I researched produced a very detailed instruction on how to use the divine power to heal the sick. This was all supported by scripture passages quoted by Jesus in the work of healing others. Their healing meeting attracted thousands of people. When the altar call was announced, hundreds of sick people would come up front to the altar.

This happened after an outstanding pastor or evangelist would give a summation of the great work of healing supported by scripture and to show what Jesus did when he healed the sick.

Then the healing prayer would begin with deep, sincere and honest devotion asking God through the Holy Spirit to remove the pain and make the patient whole again by placing their hand or finger on the pain.

These legions of healing took their group of healers to many other parts of the world and had great success as thousands of people were healed.

The Diocese of Orange has a healing program with professional healers, priests who have been trained in depth of the process of healing. They have frequent services at St. Angela Merici Catholic Church in Brea, CA.

CHAPTER 15

SUMMARY

As children of God, and God wants us to be holy, we are given many opportunities and graces to become holy as the good Lord want us to be here on Earth. Practically, the entire scripture is guiding us in this direction. In essence, the New Testament is replete with scripture telling us how to pray, act, helping self and others, how to become better persons by following the God-given plans he has for our existence.

The following steps are recommended or you can modify the steps dependant on your current spiritual progress.

- You must have a strong desire to become holy. First, you can seek the advice of your spiritual director or counselor. Otherwise, you can begin to communicate directly with God and ask Him what is His will or plan for you to become a holy person. Check to make sure you are going in the right direction.
- A considerable amount of time must be devoted to prayer. Besides vocal prayer, we can offer up our daily work habits as prayer. However, we need to have God bless and sanctify

each moment of our daily lives as prayer to be sure that each moment of our lives are laced with special gifts and graces from God.

- Being in this world of sinful temptations of a variety of pleasures, we readily succumb to pleasures. Those sinful pleasures must be eliminated, confessed and absolved to a priest.

- Ideally, we must receive the Eucharist daily, or as frequently as possible. As we are the temple of the Holy Spirit, it would be shameful to starve ourselves.

- We must bring the Holy Spirit from a statue of slumber to an active state wherein we could bring it to generate a supernatural living as God wants us to live.

- This above could be done with supernatural love that goes beyond natural love. It embodies everything that is loving and pleasing to God our Savior. It can live joyfully with any problem one may encounter. It's a love that comes directly from the heart and unconditionally accepts everyone. As God's children, it takes on the characteristic of "agape" love.

- We need to be able to feed the hungry, clothe the naked, visit the sick and the imprisoned. Helping the family, friends and their relatives can be a good start. Later, we can branch out to our church and help those people.

- We need to evangelize to tell the stories from scripture that others would listen and then act upon the story. In Philippians 4:12-13, Saint Paul tells us that being in every situation, he was totally satisfied because he learned the secret of being content in any and every situation. "I can do all this through Him who gives me strength."

- The need to take upon ourselves the suffering and even death of our Lord Jesus Christ if we are to take it upon ourselves to follow in the steps of Jesus. We transform our lives and live like Jesus. We can plainly see the beauty of His life in helping sinners in all their problems.

As we start living a spiritual life, we will be filled with God's joy and happiness. It is like living in heaven on Earth. This opportunity is open to every baptized Christian. Everyone should become a better person and live holy.

Printed in the United States
By Bookmasters